T0380701

CONVERSATIONS
WITH MYSELF

MARY LICHTENBERGER

Balboa Press books may be ordered through booksellers or by contacting:

Balboa Press
A Division of Hay House
1663 Liberty Drive
Bloomington, IN 47403
www.balboapress.com
1 (877) 407-4847

Interior Image Credit: Mary Lichtenberger

Scripture is taken from Psalm 118:24 of the King James Version of the bible.

ISBN: 978-1-9822-3398-3 (sc)
ISBN: 978-1-9822-3399-0 (e)

Print information available on the last page.

Balboa Press rev. date: 09/13/2019

BALBOA.
PRESS
A DIVISION OF HAY HOUSE

To Maria Avendaño

Mom,

Thank you for giving me life and sharing your life with me.
Thank you for your love, your care, and giving yourself to me.
Watching you praying with such devotion, at the feet of the statue of
The Sacred Heart of Jesus at the Esclavitas Chapel
I learned about faith, devotion and trusting God.

I've just realized how much I have in me from you.
Your love for gardening, pets, and nature,
Your willingness to dive into your faith is as intense
As my diving into spirituality.

Thank you for having accepted my beliefs
Even when they were different from yours.
Thank you for having encouraged me to write
And let me free to live in my world of fantasy
Even though you sometimes said, "land Marita, land!

Realizing that it is from you where my strength comes from
Gives me infinite pride that I too,
was able to overcome and walkthrough
the darkest night of my soul and the biggest losses.

Loneliness, sadness, brokenhearted, pennilessness,
devastation, despair were not enough to break me.

Because I am your daughter,
I have in me who you are.
I have your values, your hope,
Your faith and determination.

You are a woman who never complained about working
Two-full time jobs for most of your life,
To support the family and me.

You never had to preach on how important education is.
You simply led everyone in our family by example.
You got your Master degree when I was in my teens.
Not because you need a better job or a promotion;
But because of your love of learning and teaching,
Leaving us with no excuses
but to become professionals too.

What a great woman you are mom!
I love you, mom!
My biggest blessing and pride are
that you chose me as your daughter

CONTENTS

AUTHOR'S NOTE

There is a continuous dialog ongoing on my head. Most of this dialog is not flattering, uplifting, rewarding, or loving to me. I realized I have a lack of verbal resources to feed positively this internal dialog. I know I lack "talking points" to frame my inner monolog and persuade me to value, care, love, and appreciate the good person, woman, and human being I am. Even to recognize, write or say it out loud make me feel a little uncomfortable. Sadly, this is a feeling I share with some people I know.

Most of the time, I focus my attention on the source, reasons, and culture to explain this mental dialog instead of its detrimental effects on my auto-esteem, confidence, and self-love. Being as important as this dialog is in all aspects of my life, I have done little to improve this deficiency. Choices in career, employment, salary, spouse, partners, and friends depend on what we/I tell my inner self about me.

I want to nurture my inner self with a better dialog. I want to create setup phrases that my mind can use when I am not watching. A mental dialog that uplifts me, make me feel worthy, content, loved, happy, valuable. I want to plant the seed of images in my mind that refresh my soul in a day when my load feels too heavy to be watching my thoughts.

In my community, there are many homeless cats. I have been feeding some of them for years at regular hours, but they always seem to doubt if they would be fed again today. It is like something in them keep them from trusting it will happen. Sadly, I do too. As those cats, I have always been provided, generously most of the time, but I do have doubts and concerns about my provision. I want to change that frame of mind.

I started a game that consisted of guessing how Jollie, my cat, would perceive his reality. How his thinking and his internal dialog would be. This dialog, if cats talk to themselves, most probably would be one that affirms his self-confidence and his conviction that he is loved and that I care deeply for him. He has a distinctive, elegant, gracious, and firm walk, that shows off confidence. He seems to accept and know he is gorgeous and loved. He has mastered the art of let people know he is unique and that his attention is priceless for the lucky souls who receive it. He excels in the art of getting attention and affection from people that not even like cats. He sits in a place where he can be fully seen and close his eyes as if he were meditating. He waits for people to start begging his attention, a look from his green eyes. When he has received enough begging, he opens his eyes but not fully, just a little bit, like Chinese eyes. If you are lucky, he might present you with a short Meow and then leave you to enjoy his gift. Definitely, he knows that in his precious little paws, he holds the key to make me shower him with love and affection anytime he wants.

And that's exactly how I want to feel, stand, and act. Jollies' confidence is my inspiration. I do believe that the Universe, God loves me and is the Source of my supply and provision for each day of my life. I want to remember and act according to my beliefs. But, why is so hard for me to remember that the Universe cares for me and loves me for who I am? I want to stop feeling lost. How do I start believing in me and loving me and my life as it is? A good start is to feed my mind, heart, and soul with internal dialogs that lead me to a joyous, confident, and loving life. If a cat can enjoy a tender-hearted, joyful, good life, I certainly can do the same. The Universe gave Jollie his vision, insight, and understanding; surely, it did the same for me. To discover the wisdom within me and love for myself is the purpose of this conversation with myself.

How can I kick off the process of loving myself? Is there a way to lead me to a successful fall in love with myself? Any start is a good start. Even the tiniest change in my thinking, attitude, routine, or behavior is a valuable tool that can lead me to a better relationship with my inner self. I explore some line of actions to start the process.

Why do we have to have relationships that seem unavoidable that brings us so much misery, pain, shame, and guilt? Why do we have to have experiences that shatter not only our entire life but also all our world? How can we understand and accept that we have free will when sometimes, all we can see is fate in action? Whose decision is that we have to have the experiences we have? An approach to understand and to make peace with painful experiences is also the purpose of this book.

FEAR

What's happening here?
Why am I feeling this?
What is this feeling?
Apprehension? Uncertainty? Anxiety?
No.
It feels worse than that!
Is it Fear?

Fear of what?
What am I afraid of?
Why am I *so* afraid?
Of losing people who give a damn about me?
Of losing "*stuff*"?

Yes, it is possible to lose everything
I saw that happening to many, many people
In a flood, fire, explosions or sinkholes

Is it what I am facing?
Of course not!
It is just my mind playing dirty tricks to me
Ugly games.

How did I get into this corner?
Into this darkness?

I breathe slowly once
Let it go slower
Breathe again
I surprise myself realizing that
I am afraid of
Something that has not happened yet.

I look at the sky
As it were a mirror
it reflects my feelings, uneasiness, fear
Even though the dark clouds that rumble so carelessly
Sound and seem close…
They are not here yet!
Not everything is dark either
There are some cloudless, bright patches
In the blue sky…

Maybe this is just an announcement
But
What would be the message?

> *What you fear may never happen*
> *It may look close, but it is not here yet!*
> *Maybe it will never be.*
>
> *None of this is a punishment*
> *It is only a warning!*

A sweet, delicate voice dawns on me
Covers me, protecting me

Calm down, nothing to fear here!
Every challenge comes with choices.
It is only up to you to choose
Where you want to focus on.
You can focus on the sights and noises
Of an unpleasant stormy day

Or

You can focus on what you know it is true:
My endless love for you,
And the knowing that
All is well, all the time!

What if this is just a way to call your attention!
What if you are missing experiencing the "good stuff?"
What if there are lessons you can learn from this experience?
What if this experience guide you
To what your heart always knew is waiting for you.
What if this is just a gift you are having difficulties seeing?

I calm down, breathe sloooowly. Calm down. Calm down…
Knowing that whatever I focus will multiply,
I decided to center my full attention at this moment,
In the now
And in His Love.

I take a few slow, deep breaths.
It feels like my heart is opening,
As it would start blossoming
It feels good.

I open my arms widely
And whisper a prayer

I welcome You, dear Heavenly Father!
I invite You to come here,

Now!
Please! Please, God!
Enter into my mind,
My heart, and
My consciousness.

I breathe out my fear, my apprehension, and uncertainty.
I let all go.
They do not belong to me.

Thank You! Thank You! Thank You!

Peace and gratitude flows through me
I bless this experience.
I affirm confidently, lovingly

God, my Heavenly Father,
You are present in this experience.
Only good comes from You.

I let go apprehension, uneasiness… fear
I release them.

I close my eyes and in my mind
I look straight to my once feared challenge.
I talk to it serenely, calmly but firmly:
You are not a challenge anymore.
I bless you.
I rename you.
I name you: Opportunity.
I call you my good,
My God-sent gift.
You are here for me.
I accept you.
I thank you.

Like a little child,
I open my arms to receive my gift
With expectation and joy.
I open myself to the experience.

I surrender.

> I am in your hands lovingly Father
> I trust You Heavenly Father.
> Thank You!
> Thank You!
> Thank You!

And so it is.

INNER PEACE

What a gorgeous day is today!
Everything looks perfect, radiant, beautiful, and so peaceful!
I feel like life is inviting me to join this joyful experience.
I accept its invitation.
Divine Love,
This calm makes my soul aware of
Your presence in this precise moment.

My senses are intensified.
The colors of the leaves are brighter,
the flowers are glowing,
and the blue sky with fluffy white clouds
gives me a sense of freedom.
What a vision!

I open my arms and allow them to take me over.
They fill up my heart with joy!
The soft breeze embraces me lovingly,
The smell of the flowers, the trees,
the grass, and the land
perfume the air and make me feel I'm home.
The sounds of the canal nearby
and the birds gossiping among them
provides a musical background.

They whisper: You belong here.
We are in you as you are in us!

Take off your shoes,
Let the breeze play with your hair
You are with us!
You are safe!
Smile, laugh, sing and dance!
None is watching!

I do!
I do smile, laugh, sing and dance
This is what freedom means!
Freedom to be me!
To open myself to me
To enjoy being myself with me!
To openly love me
To love the journey that brought me here
To this present moment
To be who I have become

I rejoice and lose myself in this feeling
All is well!
I know it.
I feel it.
I enjoy it!

FORSAKEN

Like been lost in the middle of a lake
Like been thrown out through a car's window in a dirt road
Like the sun, moon, stars, planets rushing, fleeing from the sky
Like a leave floating downstream on a small wave crest
Feeling like there are no more left to feel
Like being in a vortex whirling unable to stop
Like keep on falling endlessly
Like being in a dream trying to run away…

How did I get here?
How all this happen so suddenly?
Was it sudden?
Is this really happening?
Is this a dream?
A really, really bad, awful dream?

I look at my face in the mirror
Red swollen eyes…
Huge, dark black under-eye bags
Puffy face,
A size 9 shoe in place of my nose…

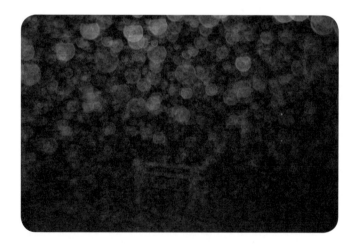

I wash my face fiercely.

NO. STOP.

I clap my hands a few times
Stop, s-t o-p, **STOP.**
ENOUGH!!!

Shake my head.
Enough! ENOUGH.
Stop NOW.

I am already hurt
I do not need to hurt myself.
I still, have *me* to take care of myself.
I am still me.

I have *me*
I can always count on me
I am worthy of me
I am worth enough to trust in me
I am worth to take care of me
I am worth enough to love me

I walk outside.
The sun is rising timidly
The clouds are fading slowly
As if they were carrying a heavyweight

The trees, bushes, flowers, grass are waking up
White ibis, ducks, herons, blue jays, cardinals
Greet life chirping loudly,
Some singing joyful, playful melodies

The warmth of a just born day greets me
The blessing of a new day embraces me
My heart skips a beat sensing the promise of
this day
My soul opens up overflowing with gratitude
A shower of goodwill surprises me

The gift of a new day!
The gift to start a new life,
TODAY

The freedom to leave pain and misery behind
The excitement of designing a brand new life for myself
The gift to give me the opportunity to choose
A partner in life worthy of my love and attention
To enjoy a loving relationship with my mother and family
A life to share with better friends

My face is surprised when a smile starts drawing on its own
My memory brings one of the couple psalms I ever learned

Today *is the day the Lord has made*
We will rejoice and be glad in it

There are certainly reasons to rejoice.
A brand new life starts for me
A handful of dreams to revisit
And re-define them, update them
Not tomorrow, TODAY
TODAY!

I bless this new day.
I am thankful for this new day.
I infuse myself in the energy of this day.
The energy of the trees, the lake, the dirt road,
The sun, moon, stars, the birds.

I let love flows inside me, around me, through me.
I welcome all the possibilities and gifts
The Universe has reserved for me.

Today is the day.
Now is the moment.
Joy is my birthright.

Only for today,
I will be happy, I will sing, I will dance.
I will welcome everything and everybody
With a heartfelt smile.

Today, and this moment is all I have
And I will enjoy it to the fullest
My heart starts humming a childhood melody

My body feels a younger body again
Today is the day!

THE POWER OF KNOWING

I am good.
I am loved.
I know I am loved.
YES!
I am adored.
I am worthy of love.
I love to be loved.
I deserve love.
I don't need to do anything to be loved.
I just have to allow me to be loved.
To be adooore.....

I am strong and loving,
I am quite a handsome little cat,
My coat is every cat's dream!
My white boots, gloves, and chest
Make me look elegant and distinct.
And my fluffy tail that I slowly swing
When I walk,
makes everyone aware of my presence.

I am proud of how I look though not arrogant.
I am fairly humble and modest.
I like myself.
I love myself.
I am wise, tender, and playful.

I don't need to do anything.
To have all my needs met.
And no.
It is not arrogance.
Nor magnificence.
It is knowing deep inside me that
I AM loved.
It is no hard to accept that
My Heavenly Father is pleased to give me his Kindom!
I just want to enjoy the moment and be happy!

It's true that sometimes
I purr or meow or
Rub my head on my mom's chin,
Lift my back
To get her attention or a treat
But it is for the fun of it!
I certainly know
all I like and more is given to me.
Most of the time, I don't even have to ask!

I also know that a few times
Things do not go my way.
The vet, the anti-flea meds, vaccines
The neighbor's dog!
Other cats trying to invade my home
Or worse,
My mom wanting to adopt one more cat!

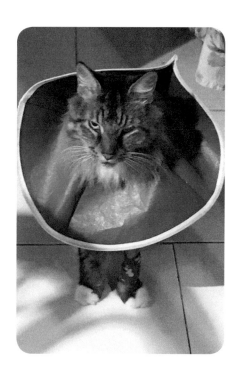

But that is just a few drops of pain and misery
In an ocean of a joyful life.

I love my life!
No needs, no cares, no wants
No rush, no begging, no tantrums
I know I am here to receive abundantly

Love, care, delicious treats,
anything I want.
when I want.
All I have to do is enjoy
while it is on its way to me.

I am here to experience love, joy, play
The good life!
I enjoy being loved.
I love to be taken care of.
I love to hear when my mom says

I am handsome, gorgeous
Her precious little thing and
That she is crazy for me.
That when I blink my almost closed eyes
She feels like melted butter in my paws…Awww!
I purr to show her I am content.
And to show her my love
I knead in her belly.

Life is certainly good.
Life is so good!!!
Look at me!
And enjoy life
This is all there is!

CONTENTMENT

What makes us want and do what we do?
What is behind our wants, needs, and desires?
Visiting some European cities made me aware once again
Of the pleasure and beauty of the simple life
Of a life with a very few good shoes, clothes, and stuff
A life of no clutter, background noise, or cheap useless products.

A life of good quality and a lot less quantity.

Of days enjoying breakfast
in a park bench with a good company.

What makes European people
Wanting to keep their forest, nature with minimum man
intrusion?

They seem to lack the need to overdevelop their communities,
or continuously destroy old buildings and rebuilt.

They seem to like, enjoy, appreciate
their old, some of them centuries-old buildings
Moreover, most of the time they rebuild them exactly
as it was before they were destroyed during the war.

They do not know what is to have their cities
under constant, endless construction all year long
for many years.
What makes them accept, like; enjoy their cities
as they are?
How can they do not feel the need for new,
modern, flashy construction?
No need for the show of seeing a building
imploding and clap at it.
What is that interest they have to preserve Nature
and include it as part of the beauty of their
design?

They keep not only their houses but also streets, cities as if they would love them!

They keep them clean; add flowers, and details just for the sake of beauty!

Why there is no need for a large manicured lawns?

Don't they have the need to show off expensive land in their wealthy cities?

Where did they leave their gloat of the power of money and income inequality and their desire to showing them off?

How come they can happily live in small places?

How come they do not need several humongous competing superstores in their cities?

And one after another store of clothes and shoes in one block?

What about huge farms where cows cannot move, walk or feed their calves?

No need to use growth hormones and free of antibiotics or other drugs in farm animals?

Don't they need several gigantic supermarkets where masters of high cuisine can choose produce from all over the world?

Most of the time they have and use fresh produce, un-waxed fruit and vegetables, mostly local

Their dishes are not just food to eat in volume and quickly.

It is art: culinary art with a design to enjoy and engage all the senses.

An opportunity of being present
at the moment
Enjoying a conversation and good company.

A moment to enjoy the simple beauty
Of fresh wildflowers just for the sake of pleasure!

A sip of good, local wine to share the pleasure of
the moment

A meal that becomes a lot more than just food!

A feast of a good moment, pleasure and beauty.

That is exactly what I want for me!
I want to start living a better life
A life of quality, enjoyment, pleasure, and beauty.

I may not be able to change the senseless, endless
Constructions and destruction of my city, street or
neighborhood
BUT I can choose a less cluttered life
Enjoy not just the food but the pleasure of engaging all my
senses
While nurturing my body, soul, and my environment.

I can start finding new friends that share my vision, my
interests
And my willingness for a good quality life.
I can start by volunteering in organizations that
Support my values and work for what I believe in.

I do want to discover within me
who I am and why I am here

And to dive into the gift of a new day
Of a new experience.

I do want to find my inner compass
To live in a state of wellness
To have a better physical, mental and spiritual health
As well as opportunities to share my God-given gifts
And lead a joyful life.

We as a society and I as an individual do have power
The power of my wallet to choose
what I want to purchase
To clutter my house and my life
or not purchase at all
and still live a good quality, simple life.

I do have the power to choose
Where to use my money
I prefer to support local farmer's markets and artisans.

I can also grow my own of tomatoes, peppers, kale
Papayas, berries, grape, and herbs.
This I can and is definitively my choice from now on.

I do have the power of my vote to choose who is in charge
of our government, cities, and neighborhoods
and to hold them accountable for their decisions.
I will stop tolerating or accepting
Their support to arms, shady decisions, endless irrational development,
and lack of sense of responsibility to their constituents

I do have the power of my voice to express
my ideas, values, hope or discontent
I will use my voice and express and advocate
the need to change what is not working for us as society
To demand a better quality of our food, water, and environment

I do have the power of my work to advocate for Mother Nature
Clean beaches, global warming, clean energy
Better policies, ethical behavior, and worthy causes

I do have the power of my craftsmanship,
my writing and photography
To work for meaningful causes:
Help veterans prevent homelessness and
Find good job opportunities.
Or teach children money and resources
management.
Help my community to access mental, spiritual
and physical health and wellness

To actively participate in pets adoption and
spaying/neutering,
Educational and recreational opportunities for
older people.
And for our youth
to learn to enjoy literary, visual, performing,
culinary.
as well as many other cultural expressions.

24

I, indeed have the power
To create beauty and meaning into my own life
And the life of my community

To wake up and live in the present moment
The consciousness that this precise moment is all we have

Contentment and a good quality life
can start with just having a pot of flowers, herbs or shrubs
that brings beauty to an ordinary moment.

FATE

What is that in life, that seems to lead us to have certain experiences?
Are we destined to have the experiences we have, and
to meet the people we have relationships with?
Is pain and misery, heartbreaks and darkest nights of the soul avoidable?
Are we free to choose our parents, siblings, spouse
And those experiences that hurt us so badly?

If we choose, how is that process?

When do we choose?

Why would I choose something
that would hurt me and my loved ones so badly?

If I choose people and experiences,
shouldn't I remember I did it?

Is there a way to escape from Clotho, Lachesis, and Atropos rule?

If I was destined to have that experience
Where was my free will, after all?

Decisions we make mindlessly, in a split of a second
Or decisions carelessly made by people we even not know
may change everything we know, want, expect, plan, or worked for.

A simple YES! to a get-together invitation can lead us
To meet the person who is going to be
The most fascinating experience or the worst disaster in our life

Why do we have the experiences we have?
Is there a purpose, meaning in our experiences?
How can I understand the purpose of needless experiences
That seems to happen completely out of the blue and totally by chance?

How can it be that a 9-ton concrete bridge falls
in top of people sitting in their cars waiting for the green light
and kills six of them
but spares my life just because I drove by a few minutes earlier?

Photo Credit: AP Images

CONVERSATIONS WITH MYSELF

None of us who drove underneath that bridge that day
Had any choice or decision in the poorly designed construction
But not only we, the ones who drove underneath the bridge
But all the community were left affected in some way.

The people that died that day were probably just having an ordinary day
Not knowing that life was about to end so suddenly
They departed without the opportunity to say or kiss goodbye
To her children, spouse, parent or loved ones
All their dreams, cares, concerns, plans died in a split second!
Too many lives changed forever in just a few seconds!

I was left with a feeling of vulnerability that causes me anxiety
A distrust that our local organizations involved with this construction
And the state and county care little for the life and safety of its residents.
Just a few minutes was the difference between life and death!
Would the six people still be alive if the light was green
and they did not have to stop when the bridge collapsed?

Was fate at work this day?

I have many other "9-ton bridges" that have collapsed in my life
And some had left me barely alive, unable to pull myself together.
Dreams, cares, concerns, plans all shattered in a split second
Unaware of from where the blow came.

And after years of intense search and asking the Universe, God
And way too many sleepless nights trying to understand
Why did I have to go through those dreadfully painful experiences?
And many, many books read trying to find meaning to what seemed
So incoherent and senseless.
I finally had my response

We choose before we come here
Before we reincarnate
Out of our free will.

And then, the whole idea depicts itself in my mind.

We get together with our "Soul-family."
And we decide what we want to experience in this reincarnation.
This soul family is not only the people
We are related to or have relationships with
But also our neighborhood, community,
our homeland and our adopted country
as well as our government and institutions
And of course our pets!

Different members of our Soul-family
volunteer to help us by creating situations
that will lead us to have the encounters
we have chosen to experience.

I understand our relationship with the Divine as the ocean
Where we, our souls, are just like drops of water in that ocean.
Love, same as in our physical world oxygen,
is what feeds and keeps alive that ocean
We all breathe in and breathe out Love,
there is nothing but only Love in that world.

Even though that state of bliss is sublime
The nature of our soul wants more, to go further
To experience something different.

I see our soul experiences the same as
the galaxies and all the celestial realm.
Each constellation is complete in itself
And has everything they possibly need
But keep on expanding and experiencing something different
Getting closer to what is unknown to them,
new black holes, or galaxies
and further to what is familiar.

I believe that the spiritual world has everything in it
But action.
Because the spiritual world is a state of being
And action is a state of doing.
Because it is not part of its nature,
Our soul craves to know how it *feels* doing.

Our physical world is so unique, so beautiful and so awesome
That our souls cannot help but want to enjoy just a little visit.

Same as we do when we leave the comfort of our home
And go camping just to enjoy nature's beauty.
We know we will not have a warm shower in the morning
Or a comfortable bed to rest after a long day of physical activities
Or that we will be eaten alive by the mosquitoes
But we go anyway because it will enrich our daily living
It will give us something we couldn't have any other way.

I imagine that when we decide we want new experiences
Is as if we take a cup of water from that ocean.

In that cup is part of my Soul-family and me,
that has decided we would share together
experiences that will complement each other.

Our free will is that
we decide to be part of that cup of water or not.
That we decide in agreement with each other
What role we are going to be part in the other soul experience.

And we all do take part in the experience
Out of love for each other and fully aware of our free will.

Our earthly experiences must be similar to children's games.

Small children are so into their roles when they are playing
That they forget that they voluntarily chose their role in the game
And so unaware that it is only a game!
To reflect in our past experiences
and trying to understand its purpose
is what makes us adults.

Looking back at our experiences
gives us perspective, purpose, and help us chose better.
Our souls want from the experience
the lessons it brings

even if it comes with some degree of pain, misery or sorrow
My experience of crossing the bridge just minutes before it collapsed
Shook my soul so fiercely
That reminded me of the value of life
Especially of my own life
Something that I take for granted most of the time.

It made me realize and appreciate that this exact moment
Is **all** we have.
There is no guarantee we'll have an extra minute for a phone call
Or to say goodbye, or I love you, or you are the most precious treasure in my life
Or to make amends or reconcile with love ones.

We waste our Nows thinking we own our future
But we don't.
We leave behind our loved ones
Because of our need of working for a more comfortable, money-rich future
That we may never have.

From the many 9-tons bridges that collapsed
in this journey called life
The lessons I like the most are:

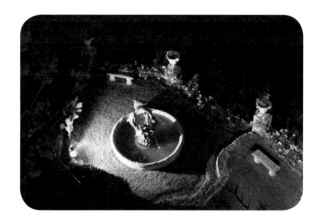

Stop just for a moment.

Look at what you went through.

Appreciate the journey,
even if was different from how you wish it were
Or more painful that needed to be.

Appreciate the people
that participated in your experience.
They were in your life
by a Divine appointment, they honored

And before you turn the page…

Take a real good, long look at your journey.

It may surprise you with unexpected gifts, or beauty

You couldn't see while traveling….

LOVING MYSELF

How does one love oneself?
How do I fall in love with myself and with my life?
What is love anyway?
How do I define love?

I sense that love is a feeling, an emotion that feeds my soul
With warmth, tenderness, care, kindness, and desire.
It makes me feel alive, hopeful, glad, and enthusiastic.
It gives me joy and makes me feel fulfilled.

To fall in love is a process.
It is unveiling the character of another being
Discovering the qualities and nature of who he is
the personality traits that make him unique.

It is to deepen my interest, curiosity,
willingness to learn more about him.
It is my need to share time, secrets, trust.

To open my heart and mind to receive and
To welcome this being into my life
To wake up desire and craving for his company

To love someone is to accept, like, admire, respect
Appreciate and acknowledge the character
Of the one, we love, just as he is.

It is to lose the hope that he will ever change or tweak
That part of his self that I dislike.

It is to admit that I love him
Not because of all I like about him
But despite what I dislike or disagree
Or have a different opinion,
or give something a different value than he does.

I am aware that I have been in love,
That I have fallen in love
And I have been loved
Many times in many different ways.
But I do not remember
Having feel love for myself
Or been in love with my life
Ever!

I realize I have loved and fallen in love with people
who had some specific physical and personality characteristics
that made me feel a strong physical, emotional and spiritual attraction.

I was willing to get to know him, respect him and admire him
for some quality that was important to me.

Being in love made me feel cherished, nurtured and protected
Filled with intense enthusiasm and expectancy for the moment when
I will be finally with my loved one.
My love grew through intimacy, togetherness, and friendship
Shared laughter, confidences, and dreams
And the knowledge that the world was a great place to be in!

Thinking about loving myself…
Do I have the physically, emotionally and spiritually characteristics
That made *me* fall in love with another person?
Do I have the character that attracted me to the people I loved?
Do I like, admire, accept, acknowledge myself as I am?

No, No, and No.
Sadly, no!
I would not be willing to go out with someone as I am now.
Physically I dislike myself terribly.
In the last years, I have gained weight consistently
And as much as I know about the devastating effects on

My physical, emotional and spiritual health
And the many ways to improve them
I have to admit I have done nothing meaningful to change my condition.

What is behind this lack of determination to lose weight?
To make myself healthier, prettier, sparkling, happier?
Where and when I lost myself that I just stop caring for me?

Emotionally I do not like who I have become.
Now, I am short-tempered and emotionally unavailable
To anyone but my cat.
Even though some time ago I recognized and accepted
The fact that I was awfully angry because all I went through
With my family, partners, and people in my life
I did understand that all the people and experiences
Had a purpose and had been chosen by me
Before I reincarnate.

Understanding, knowing and accepting this truth
Took away the bitterness I was not aware I had
It gave me peace and made my heart lighter
But I was left with the inability of tolerating
Behaviors or attitudes that I disagree with or
consider below my standards.

Instead of acting guided by my values and reason
I fiercely react before I can think.
And even when the person may have deserved that response
I still think I could have acted differently
With a little more compassion, a few dots of love
After all, who I am to judge who deserves my treatment?
Or who deserves to be treated well?
Why my reactions come before I can think?
Or my beliefs that we all deserve
To be treated with respect, courtesy, kindness, and compassion.

What is holding me to be the kind, generous, loving person
I know I am?
Why am I acting in a way I dislike?

Spiritually I don't like who I ended up being.
There is in me a lingering distrust
That I cannot identify to whom it is addressed
Is it on myself, Life, the Universe, God?

A disgusting lack of discipline to feed my spirit,
to lift myself to spirituals levels I know I can reach
because I had been there before when I was younger.

The most disappointing behavior that
Keeps me from growing spiritually to
Where I know, I could be,
Is that I am more than willing
to ride the wave of procrastination
I allow myself to be stuck and stay trapped
Knowing how to get out of that situation.

I just wait, wait and wait for a little longer
for something I know is not going to come to rescue me.

I know I am the only one that can take the first step
And by just putting one foot in front of my other foot
Only one step at a time
I can start a brand new chapter in my life.

I know and I am certain
because I had been there before
Have done that
Many, many times.

I miss being present at the moment
to feel joy and laughter coming from inside me
for no reason or purpose.

I miss feeling that confidence I had
When I knew All was well, all the time.

To be in that state of bliss took so little of myself.
Meditation once a week for a half-hour,
Awareness of the gift of a new day
Acceptance that all the experiences I had were
My own choice and were there for me, for my benefit,
Having a few breaths exercises a day
And walk for a few minutes while enjoying my neighborhood.

So little effort to receive the payoff
of living in a state of gratitude and joy!

If all it takes is nothing hard, extreme or exhausting to do
What's keeping me from taking the first step?
If I clearly remember how magnificent it feels
Why I still not doing it?
What am I waiting for?

Thinking about myself…
Is it something in me that I really, really like?

It takes quite a bit of time to realize that
Even in the worst periods of my life
I did and still do like some, a few features.

Physically, no matter how bad weight made me look,
I have always had a marked waist
And my skin, even though I never took care of it
It has made me look a lot younger, always!

Emotionally, I like the fact that I am open-minded and willing
To accept people changing for the better.

I like that I am willing and open to
Understand the intentions, motivations, and actions of others
And to change my perspective, thinking or opinion
When I understand people better.

I like that I truly believe and act on the belief
That people are born good and that
there is something inside us that
wants us to express our best.

I like that I believe that even though
pain, shame, guilt, fear are part of our experience
It is not who we are and do not define us.
I like that I believe that we can be free of all of them
when we realize who we are;
A loving, living expression of our Creator
like a drop of water on the ocean
we are exactly as the One that gave us this life
and guided us through these experiences.

Spiritually, I like that I have never lost my connection with the Divine.
Even when I walked through the alleys of death and despair
I always knew and trust there was a purpose
For me to have that experience.
Searching for the good that the experience brought to my life
Has helped me embrace it and
Be at peace with my past and the people in my life.

I like that every single time I have asked the Universe, God
why or what is the meaning of this experience,
I have always received His response soundly clear
And His answer has always, always

given me not only understanding but most important, inner peace.
I like that I have never given up on myself
That I have been able every single time
To pick up the pieces of my broken heart and soul
And custom-made myself one more time.

And now I have to make a decision.

Am I going to wait until I have all the answers
To take charge of what is not working in my life?

Some answers like why my mother and I had a very
complicated relationship came more than 35 years later.
And during all these years we missed the opportunity
To show, enjoy, dive in the love we have for each other.
All the I love yous we missed to say each other every day!
All the kisses, hugs, laughter, precious moments we refrain ourselves to enjoy!
So much life, love, time wasted just because I wanted to understand,
Understanding demolished the wall we both had built between us
but the price is unbearable.
Unreasonable
Worthless!

I have to make a decision
Today.
Now
Am I going to start living a full life today?

Anyway to start is a good start!

I can start by changing what I choose to see in myself
Just laser- focusing on what I like of myself a few minutes ago,
has changed my mood and gave enthusiasm.
And I can also use this approach with my relationships.
And my current experiences that are not what I wish they were.

I can also be more mindful and selective of my thoughts.
I don't need to change my whole life in a day.
I want to add just a good habit a week.
Today, right now
I am starting with breathing exercises just for a couple of minutes
And I'll do them before I get in bed tonight and when I wake up tomorrow
I'm writing a note to remember my commitment
and I am placing it In the lamp on my nightstand.

This Saturday I'll go for a nice walk around the lake, just a walk.
I'll take my camera in case I find an image I want to preserve.
And to anybody, I meet on my walk
I'll offer a smile and a silent blessing.
And on my way back home I'll plan for a new habit
I want to incorporate the coming week.
Nothing fancy, just breaking my current routine.
The walk will be a date with myself.
I will approach this date, exactly the same way
as I would do with a person, I have just met.

I'll look my best in my walking shoes
I'll take care of my hair, and chose my shorts carefully.
I'll start with small talk to break the ice.
I'll show my best smile and attitude.

I'll walk and look mindfully at my surroundings
I'll appreciate and silently greet
To the different forms of life I encounter
Birds, butterflies, lizards, dogs, cats, squirrels,
trees, and green grass.
The living lake with all its different creatures,
Fish, turtles will not miss my greetings.

I'll remind myself of all the blessing
I have been enjoying since I was born:

The gift of a brand new day, every day for all these years!
A healthy body that can sense, breathe, walk, think and
Has provided me all the resources to enjoy a good life.
A life full of beautiful, meaningful, joyful, and fantastic experiences.
My mother who has loved me, care for me and done so much for me
The people in my life I love and care.
My house, my home, and my Jollie
And Cherrito, Minina del Carmen, Andy, Leah, Laika, Lupita, Gringito…..

A life that has been free of illness or disease
Careers, jobs that have provided me
Not only pleasure but also an income to support me.
And the earthly possessions I enjoy so much.

During the walk, I'll do a mental checklist of
Aspects of me, and my life
I like the most, or I am proud of
I want to get to know me better
To discover who I have become.

I'll talk about the last few years
the areas in which my life or I have changed
And evaluate how much I like the new me.

I will take stock of the people in my life at this time
He ones I want to keep close to me I will thank them, bless them
And welcoming once more into my life.

The ones I want to let them go I will thank them for the lessons
they came to offer me and will bless them goodbye.

The dialog I'll have with myself will be same
As I'd have with a friend, I have seen in a long time
A dear friend with whom I'll share my hope, dreams, lessons
And my most private experiences.

I want to become, to be, my best friend
My confidant and my rock.

WOW!!!
The idea of just having this plan makes me feel fantastic.
I can feel enthusiasm and expectancy
I feel like something has woken up inside me
A boost for my heart and my soul
My body and spirit feels lighter
It feels really good!!!

Just remembering I like some aspects of myself
has sparked a warm feeling towards me.
Is this the start of a new relationship with myself?
Am I starting to fall in love with me????

Photo Credit: Alberto Diaz, MD

NOTES TO MYSELF

Printed in the United States
By Bookmasters